POWER BRAIN!

Secret Techniques To Improve Memory, Focus & Concentration

Robert Capital

has been made to provide accurate, up to date and reliable complete information. No warranties of any kind are expressed or implied. Readers acknowledge that the author is not engaging in the rendering of legal, financial, medical or professional advice.

By reading this document, the reader agrees that under no circumstances are we responsible for any losses, direct or indirect, which are incurred as a result of the use of information contained within this document, including, but not limited to, — errors, omissions, or inaccuracies.

Table of Contents

Introduction 7

Chapter 1 Memory Myths 9

Chapter 2 Memory Improvement Tips...................... 17

Chapter 3 Maintaining Your Subconscious Mind 27

Chapter 4 Training Your Senses 35

Chapter 5 Memorizing Names And Faces 41

Chapter 6 Brain Fog..45

Chapter 7 Focus In The Age Of Distractions 51

Chapter 8 Tips to Improve Focus 59

Chapter 9 Unorthodox Brain Exercises......................77

Chapter 10 Effective Learning Skills 95

Conclusion.. 101

Preview of Chakras: *Your Shortcut to Happiness!* 103

Facts About the Major Chakras 103

Introduction

First of all, thank you for choosing this book, "Brain Training".

As early as a few decades ago, it was believed that brain function peaked in a person's early adulthood and then started declining slowly, giving rise to brain fog and memory lapses. Now we know that's not the case, thanks to the extensive research in the area. But even with that reassurance, we can't stop cognitive decline.

This is mainly because of our unhealthy lifestyles and our exposure to toxins, combined with a lack of sleep. A poor lifestyle leads to loss of brainpower. And conversely, a healthy lifestyle leads to improvement in brain function.

In this book, let me take you through a myriad of brain training tips and exercises. Using them will help you improve your brain function gradually and stop cognitive decline.

So let's get started, shall we?

Chapter 1
Memory Myths

So the first thing we're going to talk about is memory. But before we get into how you can improve your memory, let's take a look at some popular myths about human memory. Understanding and busting these myths is important as it will save you valuable time when working on your brain training. It's especially important if you're someone who holds one or more of these myths. You may stop trying quickly if you think that you're forever stuck with a bad memory, but that's not the case.

Your memory can definitely be improved. Myths are only going to harm you and your determination. So let's take bust some common ones before we start. And if you hold one of these, don't be surprised.

Myth #1: There is a secret to a good memory

So many people out there think that there's a secret to improving one's memory and they want to know that secret. But here's the deal – there *is* no secret. There's no one single way to improve your memory.

There are a lot of methods and tools that you can use to improve your memory; each one works differently and improves a different part of your memory. But you can't possibly imagine improving your memory by using just one. To build a house, you need a hammer, a saw, a screwdriver, and whole lot of other tools, don't you? It's the same when it comes to memory improvement.

You have to realize that there's no quick fix or easy way to do this. It requires practice and patience.

In fact, the memory skills are not even secrets. Most of the methods have been around for more than 300 years. One method has been around for 2,000 years. No one has the right to say they "invented" a particular memory skill or that the method is a secret.

Myth #2: Memory is a thing

Nope, it's not. There is no physical part of your brain that's called memory. Memory is far from a thing; it's actually a process. Remembering things is an activity and you shouldn't think of it in terms of bad or good memory.

Remembering something requires you to think about a lot of things, and it may actually be a sum total of different memories. You may have to think about the smell, the sound, and the look of what you're trying to remember at once. Even if two memories are virtually the same, they may be remembered differently. Many times, it's not even a question of complexity. You may remember a whole conversation in detail, but not a simple melody, just because they are stored differently in your memory.

So no, memory is definitely not a thing.

Myth #3: Some people will always have a bad memory

As we've already established, your memory is not a thing. Memory is not even about ability really, so trust me when I tell you that nobody is forever stuck with a bad memory unless they have a health issue.

Some people naturally have a great memory, while others tend to struggle. But that, in no way, implies that they have to continue to do so for the rest of their lives. The memory skills that one picks up are much more important than any natural difference in memory.

Say, you have two boxes, one large and one small, and you put index cards into them. The difference is that in the small box, you put cards in a neat, alphabetical order, whereas in the large box, you just throw them in haphazardly. If you are asked to find a particular box in both the boxes, in which case do you think you'll find the said card faster? The smaller one, obviously.

It's the same with memory. One person may have a bigger box (natural memory), but if the information is not organized and good memory skills are not used, they won't necessarily have an easier time remembering things.

So don't, even for a second, believe that you're forever stuck with a bad memory. It will only stop you from trying, which is the worst thing you can do. You can always improve your memory.

Myth #4: There are easy ways to memorize

This is another myth believed by people who think there's a secret to memorization. There's no "trick", as some people believe, and good memory requires mental effort on your part. It's a learned skill, more often than not, and there is no easy way to do it.

There are memory methods and techniques that you can learn which make the process easier for you, but you still have to put in the effort. Improving your memory is like learning any other thing, like playing guitar, or driving. You wouldn't expect to learn it in a day or two, so why such high expectations when improving your memory?

You have to learn the right techniques and know where to use which ones. That is the only way you'll have a great memory.

Myth #5: Having a photographic memory is common

In movies and TV shows, we often get to see people who possess a photographic memory. They remember things in amazing detail, as if the things they see are etched on their mind. In reality, however, photographic memory is not as common as you might think it is. Very, very few people possess perfect photographic memories. Most people, who perform great feats of memory, when tested, seem to be using a wide array of memory techniques to remember things in great detail.

As we have discussed, anyone can learn memory skills and techniques to boost our memory. So if you see someone with a superb memory, don't worry. They might not have the photographic memory that you suspect they do.

Myth #6: You are too old to improve your memory

Some people often complain that they're too old to improve their memory. They think that just because they're getting old, they cannot learn some memory skills to stay sharp. It's just a myth that needs to be shunned.

Your memory can be improved at any age. Yes, some level of brain function impediment is to be expected at really old ages, but that doesn't mean you can't use memory skills. Even a 70-

year-old person who makes good use of memory skills can outperform a 20 year old who doesn't.

Myth #7: A trained memory never forgets

Another myth surrounding memory training is that once a trained person memorizes something, he will never forget it. He will remember the things he sees, hears, and does forever. That's not the case, however, because one can only remember what one wishes to remember.

Learning memory skills will help you remember more things and for a longer period than average people, yes. But you will still be prone to forgetting things eventually. With memory skills, you will dig out the required information easier when required, but at times, it will still be really difficult, and even impossible, to remember things.

Myth #8: Memory is like a muscle and exercising it helps

While repetition may help boost your short-term memory, there is no empirical evidence that it will help your long-term memory at all.

If you spend a couple of hours memorizing something with traditional rote learning methods, you probably won't remember it after a few years. But if you learn the same thing with proper memory techniques, you just might.

Simple rote learning won't solve any of your problems. So instead, you should practice learning memory skills and use them in everyday learning.

Myth #9: Memorizing too much will clutter your mind

People say that if you try to learn too much, you will have a hard time remembering anything! But trust me on this, there is no such thing as too much memorization. Your ability to remember only depends on how well organized the information in your brain is, not how much.

Practically speaking, your brain's storage capacity is "virtually unlimited", as Dr. Higbee puts it. Learning more won't disrupt your ability to remember older things. In fact, learning more sometimes helps you remember older things better. For example, people who're experts in one field find it super easy to digest new facts about the same field, and relate them to the older ones.

So never be shy of learning more. You won't run out of storage space, don't worry.

Myth #10: People only use some 5-10% of their brain power

Let's end this section with a very common myth. You must've heard this one from several people, as it's rampant in pop culture. TV and mass media are partially responsible for propagating this nonsense, too.

Truth is, there's no real research or evidence to support this statement. It's just a myth. Scientists don't even agree on how to measure brainpower and memory.

So if you have been a believer of this, update your database right now. It will do you good.

Chapter 2
Memory Improvement Tips

"There are, then, two kinds of memory: one natural, and the other the product of art. The natural memory is that memory which is embedded in our minds... the artificial memory is that memory which is strengthened by a kind of training and system of discipline."

-Rhetorica ad Herennium, 90BC

The Romans were well aware of memory systems and how to take advantage of them to train and advance their memories. If you start using them too, you will be surprised how effectively they work.

Most people don't know about these memory techniques and systems, but we have science to back them up now. For example, we now have proof that our brain processes verbal and non-verbal information through different pathways.

We also know how to preserve and improve our brain function throughout our later years, and we can use our greater knowledge of brain health combined with these memory systems to improve our memory a great deal.

Let's look at some of these memory techniques and techniques in this chapter.

The Visualization Technique

You all must have seen a professional memory performer at some point, live or possibly on some Discovery channel show. The things these performers do are just mind blowing, aren't they? They wow us with their seemingly magical abilities to remember a ton of information at once. We're tempted to believe that they have photographic memories, but in most cases, that is untrue. They all usually have average memories, but they use the Visualization and Association technique to enhance their memories to a great extent.

Also known as the visualization technique, it is a fun and powerful memory technique that you can use to remember a lot of information accurately. It's based on the simple premise that human brains remember visual information much more clearly than verbal information. For example, you may not remember all your old phone numbers and addresses, but you will certainly remember all the homes you have lived in. You will recall things in great detail, and that's because it is visual information.

This technique takes advantage of the fact that images are more concrete and easier to remember. You convert all abstract information into easy-to-remember mental images, and use these images as mental hooks of sorts to retrieve the required information whenever you need it. It does wonders for your long-term memory.

This technique works great for another reason: you are focusing more when using it. It's obvious, because when you have to create mental images of a verbal piece of information, you are forced to focus more. You also tend to go over the original material over and over multiple times, and this repetition helps you remember things better.

So here's how the visualization technique works.

Step 1: If what you're trying to memorize has some complex words that can't be easily memorized or visualized on their own, break them down and use substitute words instead. For example, if you're trying to remember that Hobart is the capital of Tasmania, the first thing you must do is break down the words. Break down Hobart into "hobo" and "art".

Step 2: Now you need to visualize the objects that your words talk about. In this case, think about hobos and artworks. Create vivid mental imagery and focus as much as you can. This will help you remember Hobart. Once you've done that, think about the Tasmanian Devil. Remember Taz, that cartoon character from Looney Toons? You can think of him too if that helps.

Step 3: In this step, you need to associate the things you want to remember. Now, you must think of a cap, or maybe even Taz wearing a cap. This way, you will remember that Taz wearing a cap with hobos and artworks means Hobart is the capital of Tasmania.

I admit that it all sounds a little daunting and even time consuming at first, but trust me, it actually *saves* you time! Once you start practicing and getting good at it, you will form connections and associations in no time.

Memory Snapshot

Everyone tries to preserve memories. Some write journal entries to describe events and things in their daily lives, others take photos and make albums, and yet others create video records. Whatever you do, it's because you feel a need to save the memories in some physical form. The problem with that, however, is that you can't carry these physical aids everywhere with you. They're precious, because they're so clear and vivid, but they're not always the most practical. So in this section, we will learn about a technique called Memory Snapshot.

We all have something called the "episodic" memory. It's the memory of events, one that keeps record of various notable events in our lives. It's a type of declarative memory that has been recognized by cognitive neuroscience.

Some of us have really amazing episodic memories. We can recall little details about not-so-significant events without any trouble. It could be a recent business trip, or a vacation from a couple years back, or even a particularly beautiful rainbow seen during childhood. And some others among us have really lousy episodic memory. We hate that we have to struggle to even recall what we had for dinner yesterday.

Well, if you're among the latter, don't despair. There's a good way to fix that. From next time, whenever you want to boost your odds of remembering an event, take a mental snapshot of it. When we don't remember things, it's mostly because we didn't concentrate enough on it to give our time to remember it. That is why we have poorly formed memories. Taking a vivid snapshot in your mind is the secret to improving your episodic memory, and to do that, you must pay attention.

For instance, let's say you're at a wedding. You may think you're observing and soaking in everything around you, but you're not actually doing it unless you're paying attention to the representative bits of it. You have to connect deeply to the situation, and really zoom in on the representative moments to create a great episodic memory.

Let's assume it's your best friend's wedding and you want to remember the couple's vows forever. In such a case, what you will do is focus intently on the couple and take a mental photograph of the scene.

Follow these steps to take a great snapshot of the memory, and use your eyes as a sort of camera.

1) **Gaze intently:** Look at the scene in front of you with utmost concentration, and hold your head steady. It's important for you to remember these details exactly, so tell yourself this firmly. Observe the colors around you, the arrangement and position of things, the dresses worn by people, and the lighting in the room. Try to soak in the smell of the flowers too, if possible. Drink all of it in, as much as you can.

2) **Blink your eyes:** Now that you've taken a thorough look at everything around you, it's time to capture the image. Slowly blink your eyes, at almost half the speed you actually blink at. As your eyes close, think of them as a shutter to a camera, and imagine hearing its sound as your eyes shut.

Once you've done all this, review the scene and replay it in your mind's eye. If the images are unclear and fuzzy, try taking another snapshot with greater intensity. Don't give up. Once you get it right, you will find it hard to *forget* the event!

Memory Systems

Memory systems are great to keep information in your brain neatly organized, like in a filing cabinet. Just like it's so much easier to find documents in a filing cabinet simply by looking at the labeled drawers and folders, using memory systems makes finding information in your brain orders of magnitude easier. You can create visual labels for things you store in your memory, and recall them at any time with ease.

Usually, the problem most of us face while trying to remember a piece of information is not that the information isn't in our brains, it's that we have no way of retrieving it. We struggle to find it amidst the chaos of all the other memories. That is why memory systems are so effective. You can greatly boost your ability to remember dates, names, abstract facts, foreign languages, definitions, and much more with the help of memory systems.

Types of Memory Systems

Let's discuss some popular memory systems or methods in this section. Here we go.

Keywords: When you want to memorize definitions or foreign vocabulary, this method is perfect for use. It makes use of a silly or bizarre mental image, associating the meaning of the word to its sound. The image, being bizarre, is quite memorable, and hence, helps us remember the word and its meaning. This method is often used in combination with other memory systems to create powerful mental images and remember complex information.

Links: When you're trying to memorize lists, stories, poems, lyrics, or any other type of reading material, even technical articles, the Link method comes really handy. All you need to do is create memorable mental images linking one item to the next one. So if, say, you're trying to remember the list of things your mom asked you to buy from the grocery store, you take the first two items on the list and link the first one to the second one using a mental image. Then you link the second one to the third, and so on. You can create a huge number of links with this method without feeling overwhelmed. Each link will remind you of the subsequent item in the list.

Peg: This method is used to memorize sequential information. You can use any of several different peg systems, like the Number-Shape system, the Number-Rhyme system, the Concrete Alphabet system, or the Alphabet Sound-Alike system. One remarkable thing about this system, or set of systems, is that you can use the same pegs over and over for different lists. You could use even hundreds of pegs at a time without getting overwhelmed, and remember as many as 6 lists with the same pegs. It's really amazing when used right.

Face-name: You must've seen some memory performers who accurately memorize dozens of names in one go without breaking a sweat. This is the technique that they use for that, and this is how they do it. They take one noticeable feature from the person's face and relate it to the sound of their name. If you see someone named Rick who has really thick eyebrows, you will always be reminded of their name whenever you see them because you relate their name's sound to a feature on their face. If you create vivid, clear labels and mental images, you will hardly ever forget people's names.

Loci or Journey: The method of Loci, also known, as the Mind Palace or the Memory Palace, is a technique that was used by the great Romans some 2,000 years ago. It's one of the most ancient memory systems, and it makes use of routes and places a person already knows to link bits of information. People frequently use the interior of a building, and it's called the Memory Palace. You might have seen Sherlock Holmes use it in the BBC TV series. He goes to his mind palace to retrieve information often.

Phonetic Number: When you need to memorize long numerical values, use this method. It makes use of sound to help you remember long numbers that are hard to remember. You start by replacing each digit in the number with a consonant, and then add a vowel between the consonants. This creates words and phrases, and once you have them down, you can easily create memorable mental images to represent those words and phrases that you've just created. One thing you need to be careful about is that each time you replace the digits with consonants, you must use a standard conversion table.

Chapter 3
Maintaining Your Subconscious Mind

There is an entire school of psychology that advocates that there is a vast region of our minds which remains outside of consciousness. This subconscious mind plays a significant role in our memory functions. In fact, some claim that all activities of memory happen in this mental area and memories only appear in the conscious mind when they are brought out by a particular trigger.

If we want to improve our memory, it is crucial to keep in mind that a big part of it is kept out of the conscious field for the most part. This is best observed when we willingly try to find a certain memory but are unable to do so. Despite knowing that it exists, we simply cannot locate it in the depths of our subconscious mind.

Although our focused efforts often provide no results, it is not at all uncommon for the particular memory to resurface on its own at some later point when we are not even thinking about it.

Everything we've experienced during our lives is safely stored and kept in this subconscious region of the brain. Many psychologists believe that a person never completely forgets anything they've experienced. Just because we are unable to recollect something, doesn't mean that particular memory is lost for good. It has just become harder to find.

Some experts also believe that although certain memorized ideas may never again resurface in our conscious mind, their existence in the realm of subconscious continues to shape our lives and dictate our actions without us even being aware of it.

The subconscious area of our mind still largely remains a mystery. There may be not just ideas and experiences, but entire systems of knowledge stored in the depths of our minds. There are numerous examples where people would suddenly start speaking and understanding foreign language(s) without knowing where they have come in possession of such knowledge.

This subconscious memory region is much like a huge filing cabinet. There is a vast amount of information in there, but without knowing where everything is stored, this information is not of much use. Sometimes things will appear out of nowhere, but it will usually be at such times when we do not have the need for that particular memory.

Finding particular pieces of memory in this filing cabinet will be easier for those memories that were given more attention when they were created and for which there are more associations that can bring them forth to the conscious part of the mind.

The more you practice, the simpler this retrieval process becomes. If a certain memory is often recalled, the time you will need to access it will gradually become shorter. However, if particular memories are not stored properly, i.e. do not have enough associations connected to them, retrieving them becomes much more complicated and time-consuming. That's why you will have a hard time bringing about those "lost" memories from a long time ago.

But even when you stop actively searching for these memories, the process continues in your brain. Once the command has been issued to search for a memory, the quest will continue for a long time even after you have completely forgotten about giving the order. Your subconscious will continue to work much longer than your willing mind.

Understanding importance of attention

Attention and association are the two most important factors for maintaining your subconscious mind. In fact, without proper attention, things are less likely to leave a big enough impression on our minds, thus rendering such memories practically useless and irretrievable.

With good attention, the images created in our subconscious mind are much more impressionable, and access to them is made much simpler. Things and ideas that were observed with little or no attention will usually make impressions so weak that even the hardest efforts will not be able to bring them to the surface.

What causes the lack of attention in most cases is the lack of interest. We usually give things and ideas we are interested in a lot of attention, but those that do not pique our interest are only given very superficial treatment. The former type of attention is known as **involuntary attention** while the latter is **voluntary attention**.

Practicing voluntary attention

To improve your memory, you must willingly practice voluntary attention. The trick here is finding a way to turn an uninteresting object or idea into something interesting. It may be hard at times, but the best approach is to try and look at an object from as many different perspectives as possible. When an old thing or idea is presented to your brain in a new way, it once again becomes interesting and attracts attention.

The first step in the process of improving your voluntary attention is arguing with yourself. This skill is indeed necessary for your development. Of course, this sounds easier than it is It will require you to do some deep thinking and fighting your initial instincts. Why would you want to put effort into turning something that is obviously boring into something interesting?

After you have made your decision, you need to really stick to it and practice hard until you master this skill. One good exercise is taking a plain, dull object and studying it in detail. Do it for as long as you have to until you can describe its every aspect. However, this may be very tiring for your brain at first, so don't overdo it. Take breaks and come back to the object when you feel rested. The important thing is not to give up until you succeed.

You could begin with a page-long newspaper article about a subject you are not particularly interested in. Try to examine it and remember how many subheadings there are, how many words are bolded, how many are italicized, how many pictures have been included and who/what is represented on them.

While this will be boring at first, you will start realizing that your brain is remembering the things you haven't even paid active attention to. This is because you are developing voluntary attention and gathering information despite your initial reluctance to do so.

Once you start developing voluntary attention, this habit of noticing small details everywhere around you will transfer to other settings like places you visit, your workplace, etc.

So, to summarize, there are three important rules when it comes to practicing voluntary attention:

1) Willingly take interest in things that do not interest you on their own

2) Look at them in such a way to be able to describe them in detail to someone else

3) Make your subconscious take notice and create impressions of these details

Importance Of Association

Creating a firm and clear impression of an idea or thing is very important when storing our memories. However, that alone is not enough. If the impression is not clearly associated with something else, recalling it will be almost impossible. The only way for something to be brought out of the subconscious mind is if it is somehow connected to other ideas or things.

The law of association regarding memory can be likened to the law of attraction in nature. The concept of association is very important in psychology, and it is widely believed that without it, it would be practically impossible for a human being to create memories.

There are two important laws that regulate the principles of association: contiguity and similarity. Regarding continuity, a particular idea is linked to the sensation or another idea which resides right next to it. In this manner, all ideas are linked to each other like a big, almost endless chain. Similarly, on the other hand, associates ideas and thoughts which are similar to one another in some way.

Understanding the law of contiguity is very important for improving our overall memory abilities. If we can link the entirety of our memory close together, remembering things will become much easier. For this reason, you should practice memorizing things in such fashion as to immediately connect them to other ideas and recollections already present in your memory.

Likewise, adopting and understanding principles of similarity will make your memory much faster and more easily accessible. Storing things and ideas in memory in such a way as to associate them with previously known facts makes later searching for them that much easier. Even if objects are not in proximity to one another in your memory palace, they are still quickly brought together by the likeness.

You can start developing your ability to remember faces by visualizing them in your mind. It is the best to start with faces that are already quite familiar, as you will not have problems recollecting them in detail. While not everyone is talented in actual drawing, you can easily draw these faces in your mind. Once you go through the imaginary list of all your friends and acquaintances, you can start trying to remember random people you've met on the streets during the day. Try to recall what little you can about their faces and then attempt to "draw" their distinctive features. Draw the shape of their nose, ears, eyebrows and so forth.

By studying faces in this manner, you will develop an interest in your mind. The task of recollecting them will no longer be a painful exercise but rather an interesting and challenging activity. By changing your approach to the matter, you will start to recognize significant improvements in the results of your recollection capabilities.

Chapter 4
Training Your Senses

Everything we know about the world comes to us through our senses. Memories are no exception to this rule. On the contrary, training your senses can help you greatly improve all techniques described in this book. The two most important sensory inputs for our memory are eyesight and hearing.

The eye

We have already explained the importance of voluntary attention when creating memories to generate long-lasting and easily retrievable impressions in your brain. Unless we combine the powers of attention with the powers of sight, we only look at things, and we rarely actually see them for what they really are.

By making a conscious effort to look at things and observe every small detail, you will quickly become very proficient in both noticing and recalling these details when required. Take this old story, which is also a good practice for training your eye for example.

A Frenchman by the name of Houdin walked past a shop window in Paris every day, and as he walked by, he tried to remember as many small objects and details as possible. He would then proceed to note down everything he observed on any particular day. When he first started, he could only memorize a few objects, but as time went by, his eyes became more trained and his attention much more focused.

After repeating this exercise for days and months, he could eventually remember even the smallest things that entered his field of vision as he quickly went past the windows. This is an incredibly powerful exercise for training both your power of perception and your memory. Additionally, it does not require any special effort. We all take casual walks or walk to and from work every day. Use this time productively and train your memory instead of just walking by.

Another good exercise is the one that the Hindus often use with their children. The children are presented with numerous small objects for a limited amount of time. They look at these objects for a while and then they are removed from their line of sight. They then proceed to write down all the objects they can remember. As the time goes by, the number of objects increases but the children's memory abilities expand with practice. So eventually, they are able to remember and write down an unfathomable number of things. This is something you can do in the comfort of your own home on your own or with your children. It is both fun and very useful for developing your perception and memory.

A similar exercise can also be performed with dots drawn on a blackboard by trying to remember the image quickly before the dots are wiped out. Then, you should try and count the dots from your mental image and see how well you do. With practice, you will be able to create more accurate mental impressions until you have mastered it almost to perfection. Thus, being able to see the entire picture in your mind exactly as it was drawn.

If you happen to love chess, you have probably seen grandmasters play simultaneously against dozens of opponents on different boards, beating them all with ease. It is because they can visualize and remember a huge number of various boards and positions. This skill is not your common variety photographic memory but rather something obtained through practice and hard work. It does not require any supernatural abilities as most human beings are capable of the same, as long as they are willing to practice enough.

A simple way to start training your eye faculties is using a regular set of dominoes. Take a quick glance at one of the tiles and try to remember the exact number of spots on it. Once you can easily do it with one tile, add another one, then another one, etc.

Your attention and focus are keys here. As we have already mentioned, it is usually hard at the beginning because these activities are not all that interesting for most people. After a while, however, your attention will be piqued by the challenge itself. Once you are able to remember five tiles, you will be interested to see just how far you can take it. You will be surprised by the potential that you most likely thought never existed.

To reiterate the main point once again, the key is in looking in such a way as to observe. Gazing without paying attention will not produce impressionable memories and memories created in such fashion will be very hard to retrieve. Use the exercises mentioned here to train your eyes always to observe.

The Ear

Apart from our eyesight, our hearing is the second most important channel through which information reaches the brain. Sight and hearing are different from all other senses because we receive impressions without direct contact with the objects that are being impressed. The information is conveyed via waves which in turn become impressions and memories.

Although the ear is the organ through which we hear, it is the mind by which we hear. Numerous sounds around us reach our ears but are never impressed on our minds. Once again, what enters our mind and what doesn't, depends primarily on the interest and attention.

The impressions that reach us via hearing are often harder to retrieve than those made by the eyes. In most cases, this has nothing to do with the sense itself but rather the lack of proper training. If we want to have a clear recollection of the things we've heard, we need to learn how to hear and listen in a right way.

If we are really focused on something, the mind will be able to pick up (and later remember) even the quietest sounds. On the other hand, even a rather loud noise can escape us almost entirely if our attention is directed wholly at some other sound. For example, a mother will usually wake up when her child makes even the slightest sound. This is so, because her attention, even while she sleeps, is greatly focused on the wellbeing of the child. A trained musician will quickly notice any wrong or misplaced tone during someone's performance. However, while people may have perfect hearing when it comes to their fields of interest and expertise, they are often almost completely oblivious of other sounds that surround them.

The key to creating impressionable memories is listening properly at all times, not only in such situations where our interest is naturally piqued. As it is impossible and would be extremely tiring to listen to everything, a good practice to develop is to either listen fully or not listen at all.

One easy way to start practicing your listening skills is by focusing on a conversation and trying to memorize the sentences exactly as they were spoken. This will help you focus your attention entirely on what you are hearing. You can start to expand this practice to lectures or even movies. Of course, it will be very hard to remember more than a few sentences at first, but with time, your brain will start to create more and more easily retrievable impressions. If you need a way to make this more enjoyable and to protect your hearing from wandering away, try to recognize different tones of voice and inflections of the person speaking. This should help your attention span.

Remember, the only way to take the full advantage of your senses is by regularly practicing them and making them work for you, by creating images and memories in your mind that you can later search for and use. Weak, pale memories, serve little purpose other than to rob you of valuable time as you endeavor to retrieve them.

Chapter 5
Memorizing Names And Faces

Although we have briefly outlined a technique for remembering names earlier in this book, it is worth examining this subject a bit more in-depth. The reason is twofold. Primarily, having problems remembering names can be very inconvenient at times, but practicing these techniques will also improve other areas of your memory.

If you have ever been in a situation where you cannot remember the name of someone with whom you have a business or professional relationship, you are well aware how embarrassing it can be. Interestingly enough, failure to remember names is one of the most common memory deficiencies in existence. Whether this is really true or it just appears so, is a topic of a more philosophical nature.

According to ancient Greek writings, Socrates was able to remember names of all of his students, despite the fact there were hundreds, if not thousands of them. Likewise, Napoleon is said to have known the names of almost all his soldiers. It seems that greatness and success are somehow closely connected to the ability of memorizing names of the people we come in contact with.

So, what is the biggest reason many of us have difficulties remembering names? Once again, we go back to the earlier mentioned theory about how our brain discriminates between what's interesting and what's not. Names on their own, are not particularly attractive. You can think about it this way: if you have ever had the opportunity to meet someone with a very strange or exotic name, you've probably remembered their name. It was interesting enough to elicit your attention. However, most names are too plain and uninteresting to leave a lasting impression.

Since names are proper nouns, they also do not create any associations in our mind. Unlike objects or ideas that we immediately connect to other things in our memory, names have no such qualities. We cannot imagine names or create mental pictures based on them alone.

One good exercise for developing your ability to remember names is by first making sure actually to listen when someone tells you their name. Pay real attention to what you are being told so that you hear it loud and clear. After hearing it, repeat the name to yourself so to create a better impression in your brain. This way, the odds of you actually remembering the name will significantly increase.

If you want to take it a step further, you can take an actual interest in the names and start exploring and researching their origins and history. While this is not something that will appeal to everyone, it can be an interesting hobby. If you research every new name you hear and connect it to newly discovered facts, the associations will be created in your brain, and will significantly improve your memory.

Remembering faces

Although remembering names and faces often go together, the two are not necessarily connected. Some people have no problem remembering faces but will have a hard time connecting a name to a particular face.

Individuals who have a professional interest in recognizing facial features, like journalists or detectives, usually have this ability well developed. For others, it once again comes back to the amount of attention you are paying.

Like names, faces on their own are not interesting. They are all quite similar unless there is something extraordinary about them, like a big scar, missing eye, or similar. These details will usually attract attention and make an impression, but otherwise, all faces are nearly identical.

However, once we reach beyond the surface and start noticing those minute details that are hard to observe at a first glance, this starts to change. Learning about physiognomy or trying to draw profiles, will help you develop an interest in these small details. You will start to realize that a nose is not just a nose. There are numerous types of noses, eyes, chins, and ears out there. Once you start looking at faces this way, you will be able to classify them, thus creating associations in your memory.

Chapter 6
Brain Fog

Brain fog, although not a medically recognized term, is often used to describe the feeling of confusion, lack of focus, and forgetfulness. It's like you can't think straight, or think at all really. Your brain feels like a puddle of goo, and you feel frustrated and even frightened at times. This is natural once in a while. Things can go fuzzy for a number of reasons, and there's no reason to be alarmed, but when you start feeling this way frequently, you have reason to be nervous. Everybody wants to stay mentally clear all the time.

Brain fog gets the best of us. If you lead a busy life, every once in a while, you may feel a lack of concentration, mental fatigue taking over, or a strange memory lapse. You may even feel like a cloud is taking over your mind, leaving your brain foggy. It's natural, and is usually caused by stress and lack of proper sleep.

In any case, however, let's take a look at some other possibilities:

- Sometimes, a temporary brain fog can be caused by low blood sugar, food allergies, dehydration, electrolyte imbalances, and heavy exercise.
- Seasonal allergies can also cause temporary brain fog.
- Women who go through menopause can also experience episodes of brain fog. In fact, it's a common symptom of menopause.
- Some drugs can also cause memory loss and brain fog, so make sure you don't take medication without proper prescription.
- Patients of cancer who're going through chemotherapy are also known to go through episodes of brain fog. It is referred to as chemo fog in their case. This is a well-known side effect.
- Another extremely common cause of brain fog is substance abuse. Any kind of substance abuse can leave you feeling mentally drained.
- While brain fog isn't an unavoidable fate for old people, it isn't rare for people of age to lose mental clarity, as they grow older. Of course, it doesn't always have to be this way.
- More serious conditions like depression, hormonal imbalance, mercury poisoning, fibromyalgia, thyroid problems and Lyme disease can also cause brain fog.

If you eat healthy, exercise regularly, and take proper sleep, you should be fine. Occasional brain fog is nothing to worry about.

What about nutritional supplements?

Sometimes, even if you're following a healthy lifestyle, you can suffer from brain fog. You try meditation and a change of diet, but the brain fog just keeps coming back.

In this case, you might be suffering from a nutritional deficiency. Yes, it's not a thing of the past. People suffer from nutritional deficiencies to this day, and it's common. Our diets are not very balanced most of the times. So you can look at some nutritional supplements to help you clear the brain fog and get back on track again.

Consider the supplements mentioned below.

Vitamin B12

This one's the usual suspect. So many people suffer from a deficiency of Vitamin B12 without even realizing it, and this is what messes up their brain function. If you're also in a constant state of brain fog and keep forgetting things, consider this deficiency. It is estimated that in the US alone, almost 40% of the adults are deficient in Vitamin B12.

This is a serious deficiency and shouldn't be taken lightly by anyone. Ignoring it can lead to a vast array of problems. Avoid mental disorders and keep your Vitamin B12 consumption levels healthy. If they're not, look for some quality supplements on Amazon. You'll get good deals there.

Vitamin B12 is only found in animal products, so vegetarians tend to suffer from its deficiency more often. Old people also suffer from it more commonly because they have poor absorption.

Methylcobalamin and Adenosylcobalamin are the best-absorbed forms of Vitamin B12.

Vitamin D

You've read about Vitamin D and its benefits in your secondary school science class probably. But just in case you haven't, let me tell you how useful it is. It can lift your mood, tackle depression, improve memory, avoid skin problems, and even improve one's problem-solving abilities. Vitamin D is also known as the sunshine vitamin because sunlight is a natural source of it.

Vitamin D deficiency is also very common, more common that you may think. Worldwide, over a billion people suffer from it, and even in the United States, over 40% of the population suffers from it.

You should go out and get some natural sunlight as often as possible, and if you can't do that for some reason, then you should take supplements. Vitamin D is rarely found in food.

Multivitamins

Multivitamins are very useful, and they're not just for old and sick people. Multivitamins can actually boost your brain function. Numerous scientific studies have proven that taking a multivitamin a day can improve one's memory and brain function. It's recommended by the Harvard School of Public Health for all adults. It acts as an insurance to fill any gaps in a person's diet.

Omega-3 EFAs

Your brain has high concentrations of Omega-3 essential fatty acids. The "essential" in their names isn't just for show. They are actually really important for the overall health and functioning of our brains, and they also crucial for a healthy memory. Sadly, Omega-3 EFAs are really lacking in our diets.

Wild-caught salmon is a great dietary source of Omega-3 EFAs, but it's not a part of most people's diets, so it's better to take supplements. It's even more important for someone with brain fog. When you pick out an Omega-3 EFA supplement, make sure it has high concentration of docosahexaenoic acid (DHA).

Brain Boosting Supplements

The above-mentioned supplements should do the trick in most cases. If you're one of the select few who just can't get rid of their brain fog even after taking these supplements regularly, it's time to try something different.

There are some supplements specifically designed to improve brain function. OptiMind is one such supplement. It boosts thinking power, energy, mood, and productivity in a person. A number of similar supplements are available in the market right now. Consult a doctor and take the right supplement.

So what's the bottom line?

Any sort of fuzziness, confusion, or lack of concentration is referred to as brain fog. It can be caused by a wide variety of reasons, including a lack of healthy lifestyle.

So if you want to avoid brain fog, make sure your diet consists mainly of unprocessed foods, you get adequate sleep, you don't take unnecessary stress, and you take the necessary nutritional supplements.

Chapter 7
Focus In The Age Of Distractions

We all live in the age of distractions. The development of numerous technologies, while undoubtedly contributing to our overall quality of living, has also created an environment where maintaining focus on one thing for longer than 10 minutes has become a real challenge.

It is true that different types of distractions have always been there, from unsolicited calls from telemarketers to your neighbors dropping by uninvited. However, never before have we been so easy to reach. Yes, terms like "globalization" and "global village" have so many positive connotations attached to them, but they may not be so positive if we consider our ability to focus.

A few decades ago, if you wanted to focus your full attention on something, you could simply unplug your phone from the wall, and it would take care of 90% of possible sources of distractions. Today, things are much more complicated.

From smartphones and tablets to regular PCs and laptops, there are so many sources of wanted and unwanted information, distracting conversations, and notifications. While we will discuss some ways to deal effectively with these distractions in the next chapter, it is important to recognize that we are living in the age of distractions, and things are not about to change for better.

There are many things competing for our attention nowadays. Some of them are more important than the others, but if we give even a minute of our time throughout a day to every single one of them, we will have very little time left to focus on what's really important. Not to mention, all these different distractions also drain our mental power even if we are not aware of it.

When the Internet and other modern technologies were making their first huge leaps forward, we were all very excited about it. Well, most of us at least. The possibilities seemed endless. From sharing information to communicating with people across the globe without having to pay anything, and having real-time updates from every corner of the world. How could this not be a good thing?

One thing that we could not possibly predict was that all these streams of information could quickly become overwhelming and distracting. So much so, to the point where we spend a greater part of our day focusing on things that have no actual relevance to our everyday lives. Not to mention, the deliberately thought-out strategies designed to steal your attention as much as possible.

If you know anything about how the Internet works, or more precisely, how people on the Internet make money, you will be aware that your attention is invaluable to them. They are not required to offer anything useful or meaningful to you. Their only goal is offering the type of content that will keep you browsing through their pages for as long as possible.

So, it is not only that the Internet and other media outlets create unwitting distractions, but there are expert teams whose only task is coming up with the ideas that are likely to shift your focus from whatever you are doing right now to what they are serving you.

This should not be understood as an attempt to demonize the modern technologies. A lot of things that were made possible because of them are useful and convenient. This is simply intended to make you understand that the backbone of the Internet today, just like anything else, is the profit. Additionally, those profiting from you doesn't particularly care about the quality of your life. They care about the quality of their own lives which is significantly improved by all of us clicking through a bunch of useless content.

Information addiction

Humans are, by nature, addictive creatures. Our habits quickly turn out into needs, and those needs often become addictions. Constantly being surrounded by endless streams of data made us information addicts.

The sense of urgency has been attached to many things, like responding to your emails or liking your friend's latest photo on Facebook. We've become convinced that things simply can't wait; if we wait too long, they will go away, disappear, or become less valuable. None of this is true of course, but if we live our lives guided by this idea, its truthfulness doesn't really matter.

Let's face it. How often do you check your phone while having coffee with your friends? A dozen? More? There are, of course, exceptions to this rule, but generally speaking, our behavior clearly displays signs of addiction. What if someone sent you a message and you don't respond right away? It's rude and unthinkable. You must be prompt.

Of course, if you carry around such a powerful source of distraction right there in your pocket, how could you possibly focus on listening to what your friend is telling you? Yes, you are hearing the words but are you really listening? Or is your brain preoccupied with thinking how long has it been since you last checked for new emails and notifications?

It is not so easy to get away from all of this. We are where we are, and we live in this period of time, with all of its perks and downsides. The only way to escape the technology and the fast lifestyle completely would be to dislocate yourself completely from civilization. If you want to be a part of it, however, you also have to accept some of it standards, rules, and norms.

Keeping the balance

However, at some point, you are allowed to say "enough is enough." You should be the one using the technology, not the other way around. If your focus is shifted every time you receive a new message or every time there is a new picture posted, then you will most certainly be missing out on many important things.

Real and personal relationships have always been at the core of our existence. No amount of technology will ever be able to substitute for that. One hour of real, close-up, and personal conversation over a cup of coffee is usually worth more than ten hours of chatting on Skype or Viber. Why? Because that's just who we are, and that's how we are wired.

On the other hand, that hour can be worth close to nothing if you are unable to give it the attention it deserves. People will always notice that your focus is divided between them and your phone. And they will take offense. Even if they do it themselves, they will still find it insulting that you are unable to spend an hour listening to them without constantly checking what's going on elsewhere.

So, while you cannot just say "no" to technology (nor should you), you most certainly can "disconnect" while meeting with a friend who needs your ear. Nothing bad will happen, the world will not end, and even if it does, you finding out about it on Facebook will hardly make any difference.

The family life also suffers because all these distractions. Instead of sitting down for a family meal, these days parents and children gather around the table with their "smart" devices and hardly even recognize the existence of others in their proximity.

Succumbing and accepting that this is just the way things are today is easy, but it will not solve anything. You need to take control and establish at least a semi-balance. There are times when you need to unplug and connect with those closest to you. Focus on them and their needs. Your friend from Australia will understand that you couldn't instantly respond to their messages because you were having a dinner with your family. He will not hold it against you.

Even if your job requires you to stay online pretty much all the time, you need to make your bosses, partners, and clients aware that you can't actually stay connected 24/7 - even if they expect it from you. Calmly explain to them and make them mindful of the fact that there are periods in your day reserved just for you and those closest to you. Again, most of them will understand. If they don't, well, it may be time to cut them loose. Do you really want to spend your entire life on the grid while those genuine, and personal relationships deteriorate beyond repair?

No doubt about it, this takes courage. It takes a certain level courage and determination to get out of the pack, so to say, and establish your own rules and norms concerning your availability. We've been implanted with certain expectations which, with time, have turned into rules. But just because something is a "rule" doesn't necessarily mean it has to be right.

The Internet and other modern technologies are not big bad wolves looking to devour you. However, they can certainly eat into your focus, energy, and personal relationships. The first step in battling this is recognizing that we live in a society whose norms are somewhat skewed in that regard. After you've come to terms with this fact, you can start changing things for the better.

The following chapter contains some very useful advice and exercises on how to improve your focus and disconnect yourself from the distractions, at least from time to time.

Chapter 8
Tips to Improve Focus

Wherever you go in life and whatever you choose to pursue, your focus will decide your success. Focus is one of the hardest things to achieve. Our minds are like wild horses, as the Bhagavad Geeta says. They always want to go in ten different directions, and unless there's a charioteer to rein them in, they will go off to do whatever they want to. It's the same with our senses. We need to rein them in and take control, or else they will take us places we don't really want to go.

Let's take a look at some tips to improve focus in this chapter.

1. Practice meditation.

I can almost hear you go "duh!" at this moment, but I had to mention this. Meditation is the go-to way to improve focus, and it's *so* important.

Ideally, you should take out some time for meditation and use it exclusively for meditating. But most of us cannot do that. Well, the great thing about meditation is that you don't *have* to allocate time to it. You can practice it any time you want. Start by taking deep breaths and focusing on the air entering and leaving your lungs. Focus on the air and feel the way it touches your upper lips and nostrils; feel it touching the back of your throat and feel your lungs inflate and deflate. Do nothing else but just focus on this motion for a while. Don't try to go thoughtless in the beginning. You won't succeed in all probability. At this time, there's usually an endless and absurd chain of thoughts that your mind goes through. It becomes slightly restless and starts wandering off, but you don't have to try too hard to hold it back. Just nudge it whenever it tries to drift away and bring it back to focusing on your breathing. This will calm down your circulatory systems, and you will also feel a sense of peace and calm. You can do this anywhere and at any time; literally all you have to do is breathe. The next time you go out on a commute, wait for your code to compile, or wait in a life, try this.

2. Listen to music.

When I say listen to music, I mean you really have to listen to music. It's something that you need to be focusing on, something that you're doing as a primary activity. If you're exercising or working on something else while listening to music without paying any attention to it, it won't do you any good. Listen to good music and focus on it.

Most people feel its power when they first start playing some instrument. That's what happened to me, too. When I started playing the guitar, I started paying more attention to the music I listened to, and with time, I could listen to each instrument's individual notes. I could hear the base lines, the rhythms, the lead solos all being played in sync. This opened up my ears and my brain to a lot of new things. I started enjoying a lot of new music that I never listened to before, and I could also focus on a single instrument at a time and tell what exactly was happening at a particular moment.

Listening to music is another form of meditation. You clear your mind off of everything else and just focus on the music. There's no clutter in your brain and all you can hear is the song. It adds a whole new dimension to the way you approach music.

3. Work when you are most comfortable.

Not all of us feel most productive or comfortable at the same time of the day. Some of us work better during the day, while others feel more comfortable working during the night. While you should certainly get good sleep during the night, it's okay to prefer working during late hours. Find the time you feel most productive, and then utilize that time doing what you consider most important to you.

4. Divide your goals into smaller chunks that can be readily achieved.

While having an end goal in mind is great, it's not enough to keep you motivated. We often find the initial drive to do things but soon start losing focus and get frustrated with what we are doing. This is because our goals start seeming too big and unachievable. We don't see immediate results, and it makes us question our progress. It's very demotivating. A great way to counter it and stay focused is to break down our goals into smaller targets that are more readily achievable. Set tight (but realistic) deadlines for yourself, and then check off items from your list of things to do. You will feel accomplished and powerful.

5. Start fasting a bit.

Heavy food tends to slow us down and makes us feel lazy. We've all felt it at some point of time, haven't we? After a solid meal in the afternoon, we feel like laying down for a nap sometimes. It's because the brain directs the blood supply towards the stomach to speed up the digestive process, thus making us feel sleepy.

Intermittent fasting can help you combat this. It has a lot of other benefits too, when done in moderation. When you do a bit of fasting, your metabolism tends to speed up and you stay more alert; you also stay in shape. Just try not to starve yourself, okay? Death can be kind of counter-productive to what we're doing here.

6. Practice delayed gratification.

People who can delay gratification have a higher chance of succeeding in what they set out to do. There have been countless examples of this, and it will continue to be the case. There was even a TED talk on this topic. People tend to focus on the bigger picture when they're not distracted by the greed of immediate gratification. They keep the bigger goal in mind and don't get distracted by little things. You should also practice delaying gratification in your day-to-day life. With time, you'll find it easier to say no to that last donut, to not have fries with that, to throw away that last cigarette, to say no to that extra cheese, stuff like that you know. You will have more of "Yes" in your life and more time to do the right things.

7. Force yourself a bit; don't force yourself too much.

There are times when you should be working and times when you shouldn't be. The former is when you're feeling kinda lazy and need some extra push to get started. It's okay to push yourself a little and get in the flow. We all need some extra motivation at times. However, at times, we feel too mentally absent to do anything. We hit a wall and our brain refuses to do anything, no matter how hard we try. It's times like these when you should let go and stop forcing yourself to work. You won't achieve anything or do anything productive even if you work during this time, so it's better not to. Go do something else during this time, ideally something completely different from what you were originally supposed to be doing. Blow off some steam and then come back to the original task.

8. Wear light clothes whenever you can.

Have you seen any sadhus (hermits) practice meditation? They all are wearing such light clothes. That's because having good ventilation is healthy. Whenever you can, wear light clothes.

9. Sit with Mother Nature every once in a while.

Try and go out to be with the nature whenever you can. It can be as simple as going to the park. Just lie down and listen to the birds singing, the twigs cracking, and the wind swooshing through the tree branches. Maybe go by a riverbank and hear it babble over the stones, or go to the beach and listen to the waves crashing on the shore. All you have to do is sit and pay attention. Let yourself immerse in the beauty of nature, and it will calm you down greatly. You will be able to focus much more when you want to.

10. Give yourself some buffer time.

When you finish a piece of work, give yourself some time to breathe. Lay back for a couple of minutes and let yourself unwind. Breathe deeply and feel the stress in your body disappear. It prepares you for the next task and prevents fatigue.

11. Some things just take a minute. Don't procrastinate them.

We feel really tempted to put off the things that are really tiny and insignificant for later. We tell ourselves that there's plenty of time to do them and that we can easily do them later. It's only when they pile up and start stressing us out that we think about them again. Before these things start burdening your mind, finish them without any delay.

12. Exercise your mind daily.

Get your creative juices flowing by engaging in some passionate discussion with others and building things you like. Solve some puzzles and do that Sudoku if you need to; just don't sit idle. And no, meditation is not keeping your mind idle, just an FYI.

13. Exercise your body daily.

Take some time out of your daily schedule to exercise your body. You don't have to be really hardcore and become the next Ronnie Coleman. Just remember to treat your body well and stay in shape. Your body should never be a liability to you.

14. Remove yourself from distractions

We live in the day and age in which distractions of all kinds are just a phone call or mouse-click away. Staying focused on even the most exciting of tasks can represent a real challenge. You may think that you are strong enough to avoid these distractions by the power of your will alone, but in reality, most of us just aren't.

When you want to really focus on something, you need to remove any potential distractions as much as possible. Put your phone in airplane mode so that no messages or calls can come through. Log out of Facebook and even your email if it is not required for what you are doing at the moment. Devote your full attention to the task at hand for the next hour, two hours, or however long you plan to work on it.

If you don't believe me, try and time yourself next time when you are doing something with all distractions present. Write down the time you spend reading an interesting article or chatting to a friend, all the while you are supposed to be working on something and focusing on a task. Even if you know you are timing yourself, and you could easily cheat, you will quickly come to realize that the distractions are just too powerful to resist. Cut them off entirely, as often as you can.

15. Start your day with some peace and quiet

I realize this can be hard for some people, especially those living with families, but starting your day in a proper way is of the utmost importance for your focus throughout the rest of the day. You can try waking up before the others in your household. Losing 15 - 20 minutes of sleep is well worth it if it gives you time to start your day peacefully and collect your thoughts.

Have a relaxed cup of coffee and do some reading. Read the morning newspaper or a few pages from a book. It will not only help you focus your mind, but it will give you the added benefit of finding some time in your busy schedule to do something you actually care about.

16. Set important goals for every day

There are so many things one needs to get done every day. Some of them are quite important, and others are almost trivial. However, if you don't make a clear distinction between them, your attention will always be divided, and you'll spend your days running around from one task to another, trying to cover as much ground as possible.

Instead of doing that, each morning after your personal time, set a few important goals for that day. You can write them down on a piece of paper or make a strong mental note. Either way, make these tasks the focus of your day. Get to them one by one until you've completed the list. After that, you will feel happy and accomplished, and you will usually have plenty of time left to do some of those smaller, less important tasks.

17. Alternate your focus

Focusing on one thing at a time is good, but it can also become somewhat boring and tedious as you will sometimes spend hours doing the same thing. To prevent your brain from going on autopilot without dispersing your attention too much, you can alternate your focus between two different tasks.

This way, you will work for 15 minutes or half an hour on one task, and once you realize your attention and interest are declining, you can move to the second task. Repeat the alternation procedure until both tasks are completed.

You will not only get everything done with better than expected results, but you will also feel much less tired at the end of it all.

18. Get in a habit of reviewing your work

Doing a quick review of things, you've done or failed to do despite planning at the end of every week, can be a great exercise for your focus. Sit down and really think about everything that happened during the past week. Were you able to complete everything you wanted? If not, why? What were the things that preoccupied you and stole your attention? What can you do to change things around?

19. Remove the sense of urgency from everyday things

Living in the fast, modern world, we've become accustomed to everything having a sense of urgency attached to it. We feel the need to answer immediately any email we receive, and to respond to any tweet or Skype message in a matter of minutes. The world keeps coming at us with trivial things, but making them feel as if they were of the utmost importance for our existence.

To improve your focus and clear your mind of distractions, you need to get rid of this notion. Of course, you will answer all the emails, respond to all the messages, but why does it all have to be right now? If you lived thirty years ago and received a letter from a friend or business partner, in most cases you wouldn't sit right down to write a response. You would wait until you have some free time so you can really focus on writing and do it properly.

The modern world has implanted us with this fear that if we don't answer right away, people could think less of us or we could miss out on something important. While this is not true in at least 95% of cases, we are still afraid that this particular message could be in that 5%.

It is not easy to get rid of this feeling as, by this point, it has largely become a part of who we are. You need to do it willingly and consciously. Force yourself to postpone answering to that email or ignore the SMS you've just received. Unless however, it is something really urgent. Let it rest for a few hours and only respond later. As you start doing this more, you will come to realize that nothing bad will happen because of it. Everything will still be the same, the work will get done, your friends will still talk to you just as before, and you will not miss out on anything. It's a promise.

20. Information is good; too much information is a burden

We are being bombarded with information from all sorts of sources. While there is no denying knowledge is power, there really is such a thing as too much information. At a certain point, it becomes impossible for our brain to keep up with all of it and this results in distraction and loss of focus on what's really important.

Once again, the reason we try to store so much information is - fear. The majority of data we consume throughout the day doesn't contribute to our life in any meaningful way. It doesn't make us happier or even make our daily life easier. We are simply fearful that by skipping on a particular piece of information, we might miss out on something big, important, or actually valuable.

Just like with the false sense of urgency, this is another fear that doesn't have a real foundation. Trying to keep up with all daily events so that we do not seem ignorant or miss an opportunity takes a real toll on our brains. If anything, it is exactly the opposit.: By removing all this unnecessary information from our lives, we will have more time, energy, and mental focus to use on something productive and useful.

21. Un-clutter your working space

Clutter is bad for your focus, plain and simple. A cluttered working environment is full of distractions waiting to happen. In the pile of papers, documents, and paper mail, there are numerous things lurking, just waiting for the right moment to distract you and seize your focus. Don't fool yourself into believing that you will resist the distractions, because you won't. Succumbing to them is often pleasing and a welcome change from whatever you are doing at the moment.

Instead of trying to fight off these distractions, why not simply remove them altogether? Create a clean, tidy workspace where you will be able to focus fully on your tasks one by one, without being interrupted. Ideally, you should even block out any outside noises and cover them with music instead - just makes sure the music itself is not distracting.

While at it, you should also consider cleaning up your computer's desktop. If you are like the most of us, there are numerous documents, pictures, and folders just lying around on your desktop. These not only make it harder to find things you actually need at any given moment, but also threaten to grab your attention and take you down the path completely opposite to what you had planned for that day.

22. Switch to a lower gear

Everything we've mentioned in the earlier advice boils down to one thing: we live our lives in high gear, always trying to get as many things done in as little time as possible. If you want to better your focus, you need to move away from this mindset.

By rushing things, you may get more done, but the quality of what you do will undoubtedly suffer. If you are trying to squeeze too many things into a small timeframe, you simply won't be able to give any of them the focus they deserve. Not to mention that it will be nearly impossible to enjoy doing even the things you are supposed to like.

It is necessary for you to realize and accept that living life in a lower gear is not only much more enjoyable, it also helps you produce better results. Just as you enjoy a good meal more when you take your time chewing and really tasting it, so will you enjoy your everyday tasks more if you give them the necessary attention and produce results that you are satisfied with. In most instances, if you feel like something is well done, others will be thrilled with your work. Since we are often our harshest critics, learning to do things in a way that make us proud of our work will usually be far above what anyone else expected.

Of course, slowing down doesn't come easy. Once again, there is fear that we couldn't keep up with our numerous obligations if we took a step back. Will we be able to pay all the bills, meet all deadlines, and make everyone happy?

The key is taking control. You can schedule your meetings better, so you don't have ten of them in one day. You can push the limits on certain projects. No one will think less of you for that. If anything, they will stop taking you for granted and will instead see a person who knows what they are doing and is perfectly aware of their capabilities. Not to mention, improved results and your increased enthusiasm will more than make up for the extra few days you took so you could really give that project the attention it deserves.

23. Stop stressing over things you can't control

Even if you manage to organize the things in your life just the way you want them to be, individual events beyond your control will often act as disruptive forces in your order. They will just happen without you wanting or expecting them. There is nothing you can do about it.

The most important thing in situations like that is not to stress about them. Stress, is the worst possible thing for your focus. It will disrupt your thought processes, make you unable to focus on tasks at hand, and your results will suffer.

Instead of stressing, try to accept that you will never be able to control everything that happens to or around you. Although this is common knowledge in a way, most of us are still prone to getting annoyed when things don't go as planned. If you've adopted meditation as a part of your daily routine, as suggested earlier, this can help you deal with these unexpected events.

You need to always try and put things into perspective. For example, if your car broke down, it may seem like the end of the world at the moment, considering you were planning a weekend getaway and this may have ruined those plans. Take a step back however, and try to look at this incident a year later. It will be just another funny story to tell your friends over a dinner. So why stress about it now and let it disrupt your mind?

Take things in stride. If something happens and you had zero control over the event, simply shrug it off and try to laugh about it if possible. You know it is not the end of the world, so don't let your frustration get to you and turn a small, irrelevant thing into something that will influence all aspects of your life.

24. Learn to let go of certain goals

If there is anything that will reduce your focus and occupy way too much of your mental capacities, then these are tasks and goals that you keep trying to accomplish despite knowing that it is nearly impossible.

Yes, you need goals to succeed. Yes, you need to focus on one goal at a time to give it your best. All this holds true. But sometimes, pursuing a goal and giving it way too much focus and time is simply not worth it.

If there is a goal like that in your life, it is time to let go. It's been time for a while now, and you know it, but you feel like you will be letting yourself down if you drop a goal. What you need to realize is that goals shouldn't be your fixation but merely guiding lights on the way to your final destination - and that destination is a happy life.

If one of your goals takes all your time and focus, then you simply have nothing left for the rest of them. It is one thing to give something difficult more time and effort; some things simply will require more of your dedication. But chasing something without any visible results just because it is on your list of goals, this you should never do.

Just remove that particular goal from your list and your life and instead focus on the things that you can achieve. There is no doubt this will help you live a much happier and stress-free life.

25. Pay attention while reading

Back in a day, only the rare (and lucky ones) knew how to read. Luckily, we live in a time and place where reading is perfectly normal. In fact, it has become so standard that we have perhaps taken it a step too far.

Is it because of the fast-paced life or the low average quality of reading materials we are offered on the daily basis, but the fact is that we've become accustomed to reading without focusing or paying attention to what we read.

These days, very few of us have the patience and mental focus to read long books and articles. We are perfectly satisfied with skimming through short blog entries and news headlines. We gather short, incomplete pieces of numerous information, instead of focusing on the real message.

To be able to focus on reading, especially if reading books, you will need to get rid of all distractions and really immerse yourself into the pages you are flipping with your fingers. Although it may seem like a somewhat outlandish idea, you should really give it a try every once in a while. You will realize that focusing on a good piece of reading is not that hard at all if you willingly remove everything else that could distract you.

Chapter 9
Unorthodox Brain Exercises

To make the best of your brainpower, you have to give your brain new experiences. It's how your brain develops and produces natural brain nutrients that help memory. In this chapter, we shall look at some unconventional exercises for you to try. They will help you combine physical senses with the emotional "sense", and make your brain cells stronger and more resilient. Try these when you're down or during your morning routine. They work like cross-training for the brain, and you will definitely feel the difference.

1. Shower with your eyes closed

This exercise is meant to enhance your other sense by not using one sense, the sight. When you're unable to *see* things around yourself, your brain will be forced to use other senses to feel things around you. You will notice textures and shapes around you and relate them to objects in a way you might not have done previously. Try and locate the taps just by feeling them out and not using your sight. Adjust the temperature and then take a bath with your eyes closed.

2. Brush teeth with your non-dominant hand

Almost every person relies on their dominant hand to perform most tasks that involve using hands. The dominant hand has more strength, more dexterity, more agility, more everything, so using it exclusively for so many things makes sense. But in doing this, we tend to limit our brain function sometimes. But when you use your non-dominant hand, you trigger the expansion of parts of cortex. This expansion is rapid and substantial, giving your brainpower a boost. So try brushing your teeth with your non-dominant hand every now and then. Heck, try doing other normal stuff with your non-dominant hand. Peel a banana or an orange, use your computer's mouse, pour your coffee into the cup, or anything else you can think of.

3. Pick your clothes with your eyes closed

Picking up your clothes in the morning using only your sense of touch is a great memory-boosting activity. Figure out the type of clothes you want for that day (rough, silky, etc.) and try to pick the items of clothing by touching them. Don't use just your hands but also other areas of your body rich in touch receptors, like cheeks or lips. This exercise will help develop the parts of your brain in charge of the touch and will force you to use the senses which are often neglected in creating memories and impressions.

4. Switch around your morning activities

When you try a new activity, your brain activity increases in certain areas, and studies show that these tasks affect large regions in the cortex. When things become routine and mechanical, the brain activity tends to decline. We start taking things for granted and don't pay enough attention to the activities we're doing. To change this, you should not fall into a rut and keep things fresh. If you get dressed before breakfast usually, try doing it after at times. If you walk your dog on a particular route daily, try changing it every few days. Browse through new TV channels and watch programs you've never watched before. The point is to give your brain something new to do and think about.

5. Turn familiar objects upside down. Literally.

Here's another fun exercise. You must definitely be wondering how this one helps because it sounds completely silly, right? Well, it so happens that our brain is very quick to label things when we see the, right-side up. It instantly tells you the name of the object and moves on, diverting your attention elsewhere. This doesn't happen when the object is upside down. In that case, your brain carefully processes the colors, shapes, and relationships of the puzzling picture before it. So take everyday objects whenever you're free and flip them over to see how they look like upside-down.

6. Switch seats at the table

We usually have predetermined seats on the table when we sit together with the family to have a meal. Everyone has their own favorite spot, and that's the way it tends to stay for long periods in most families. You should change this and switch seats with someone on the table. It gives you a new perspective on things in the room. You see people from different angles, and even the way you reach for things on the table changes. It's a refreshing exercise.

7. Read differently

Silent reading uses completely different brain circuits than when you're reading aloud. So in this exercise, I want you to read in a way different from your usual method. You can do this with a partner, where you both take turns to be the reader and the listener. It's also a great way to spend quality time together.

8. Eat unfamiliar foods

This exercise makes use of your olfactory senses. You see, whenever you eat something, a different combination of receptors is activated in your nose to distinguish the odor from others. It tells your brain what you're eating. That's why you can't taste things properly when you catch a cold.

Studies have shown that the olfactory receptors have a direct link to the emotion centers of the brain. This can trigger unexpected feelings in a person when he smells something different. In this exercise, you will need to try an unfamiliar cuisine. Browse through different seasonings, vegetables and packed goods to get a feel for the cuisine. You can also ask the storekeeper to teach you how to make some other items that are more unfamiliar.

9. Look for food that might rekindle your memories

Food can be a very powerful stimulus for your memory. By eating a particular food connected to some part of your life, different memories from that period will come knocking. For example, tasting food that you've enjoyed a lot as a child (like hotdogs or pancakes) can bring back all sorts of memories from that period, like playing with your friends, and having a great time with your family.

Similarly, eating a special food that is somehow connected to an important event in your life will often rekindle the memories of that occasion. For example, try to recreate the dinner when you proposed to your wife. Apart from the food alone, recreating other sensory inputs, like smells or setting of the place, will help reinforce the memories that come back to you.

10. Make a new connection with your nose

We learn to associate various odors to different events or experiences in our lives. An example of that is your morning coffee. You won't remember when your brain started associating the smell of coffee with mornings, but that's how it is. This exercise helps you develop new habits by associating them with an odor. Take an extract of any odor you like, say citrus, and keep it near your bed. As a week or two pass by, you'll start to relate it to mornings. You'll inhale it when you wake up every day, and this will create new neural pathways.

11. Open the car window

When going out in your car, open the window and try to recognize all new sounds and smells on the way. Your hippocampus processes memories in the brain, and it's really good at creating mental maps with sounds, odors, and sights. This exercise will provide the hippocampus with more raw materials to create mental maps.

12. Take a new route to work

Many of us commute to and from work. This time is usually lost as we spend it doing nothing productive. However, you can change that and start utilizing it to develop your memory. One good way to do so is taking a new route to work. Keep the window open if possible and pay attention to all the new details you will notice along the way.

Having a routine is bad for your brain because it dulls your senses. When you take a new route, the brain will become fully active, especially if you pay attention, and will chart a new map in your mind. It will also take notice of all the new sounds, smells, and sights along the path.

13. Wear gloves while driving

By wearing a thick pair of gloves while driving, you will dull your sense of touch. Because of this, you will be forced to rely on other senses, activating different parts of your brain. Once again, you will break the routine and will have to focus a bit more on what you are doing. Of course, only do this when driving conditions are favorable.

14. Play with spare change

When you use your sense of touch to identify and differentiate between objects, the cortical areas in your brain are activated. These areas process tactile data and this leads to stronger synapses. This is because our brains usually rely on visual information to distinguish between things. This exercise also gives you a feel for how blind people read Braille letters. Their brains simply devote more neural pathways for processing fine touch.

Here's what you need to do. Take a cup and fill it with coins. Place this cup in your car's drink holder and whenever you stop at a spotlight, take a coin out of the cup and try to identify it by just feeling it. You can do the same exercise by carrying coins in your pocket wherever you go.

15. Try to walk as much as you can

Driving to work may be convenient whether using public transport or your own car, but it is not the best way to develop your mental synapses. Make it a point to walk at least part of the way to work every day. If you commute, get off the bus a couple of stations before your destination and walk the rest of the way. While walking, pay attention to everything that happens around you: smells, colors, chatter, birds singing, etc. Let all your senses participate.

While commuting, try to read something that is entirely new to you. Don't read the same newspaper or magazine you've been reading for the past five years. Pick something completely novel in the morning and see where it will take you. As you read, think about images or ads before your eyes and try to create different mental pictures of you in the pictured or described situations.

16. Scan at the supermarket

The sole purpose of this exercise is to break out of a rut and experience something new. You see, shopping at a supermarket is a very calculated experience. Things that the store profits at the most are usually placed at the eye level, so you don't see everything when you're shopping. In this exercise, all you have to do is look at the various shelves in the supermarket thoroughly and pick up any unfamiliar items. The item doesn't have to be something you're going to buy. The point is to break out of the routine, so just read the ingredients or anything else when you pick it up, and then put it back.

17. Do an art project in a group

Art is related to emotion, it's an outlet for emotion. You must have heard of this, right? It's true, because the emotional and nonverbal parts of the cerebral cortex are affected by art. A logical line of thinking with linear ideas is executed very differently by the brain that art. When you're creating art, you draw information from parts of your brain that are interested in colors and forms, even textures. So in this exercise, I want you to create a group of people and ask each person to draw things. They can be associated with seasons, emotions, or even a current event.

18. Play "10 Things"

This is a game that children play sometimes. It's actually a great way to force your brain into thinking new ideas, which keeps it strong. For this exercise, all you need is a few people and some ordinary objects. When someone gives you an object, you have to list down 10 possible things that this object could be. For example, if you get a fly swatter, you might think of it as a tennis racket, a baseball bat, a shovel, a violin, and much more.

19. Make more social connections during your day

Social deprivation can prove to be very harmful for your cognitive abilities, and this has been proven by scientific research repeatedly. In this brain exercise, all you need to do is interact with more people than you do normally. Buy a drink from a person instead of buying it from a vending machine. Pay the clerk at the gas station instead of swiping your credit card at the pump. These little interactions can keep your brain healthy.

20. Rearrange things at your desk

As we've mentioned, the routine is one of the worst enemies for your memory. It allows you to act on instinct, without having to put any real thought into what you are doing. And for many people, the routine is more present at work than anywhere else. However, you can still make an effort to change that a bit.

You can start by deliberately rearranging things on your desk. If you've worked at the same desk for a while, you probably know where everything is without even looking. This means that you don't need to activate your brain or your senses when looking for that stapler. However, if you move everything around, all of a sudden you will have to actively search for things, which will put your brain in action.

Another thing you can do is changing your daily routine. Most of us are used to doing things at the office in a certain order. For example, quick coffee, checking and responding to emails, calling clients, etc. Try to shake things up a bit by doing them in a different order and see how that works for you. Some "disorder" can be a good thing.

21. Bring someone new to work

Taking someone else to your workplace can be a very refreshing experience. It can be your child, partner, friend, or even just an acquaintance. The importance of this exercise is in realizing how new people react to the environment you take for granted. They might even point out some things that you've been passing by for years without even noticing them.

Introducing your friend to coworkers will also help you build more connections and should prove beneficial for your name-memorizing skills. For some reason, our brain takes a better impression of someone's name when we introduce them to another person than if you were the one to meet them yourself.

22. Brainstorming

Although you can exercise brainstorming anywhere, the working environment is probably the most suitable for this type of activity. While brainstorming, new associations are created in your mind which is of the utmost importance for your memory (as explained earlier).

This exercise works the best with a group of four to six people, where one person is made a "facilitator." This person takes notes, presents the problem at hand, and guides the process. The rest of the group needs to offer as many ideas as possible that they feel could apply to the problem.

The idea of brainstorming is not to give well-thought out or polished suggestions but rather unrefined mind "gems" which can be further processed and turned into something quite useful.

By quickly reacting to others' ideas and creating your own, you "teach" your brain to make quick association bridges between different thoughts. Sometimes you will even end up connecting things you'd never think could stand together. By not over-thinking, you allow your brain to work freely and unrestrictedly.

23. Mental breaks

Your brain needs its "down" time, just like your body. This is particularly the case if you work it hard during your work day. Taking short breaks away from your job will help you return to it more focused and ready for new challenges. If at all possible, take a few 15-minute breaks during your workday and take short walks outside away from all the tasks. Let your brain focus on something else, be it the nature around you, children playing in the park nearby, or whatever else. The important thing is to let your senses take over during this time.

24. Random players chess-game

Although this may seem like a strange idea at first, it is actually a great one for developing your memory abilities. Even if you only know very little about chess, you can still profit greatly from this exercise.

The setup is simple. A chessboard is placed somewhere at the office where it will not be disturbed. The moves are made random, by anyone who feels they have something to contribute. There are no winners or losers in this game as the whole point is to make you think about the game, visualize it in your mind, and come up with potentially good moves in the current situation.

This type of exercise will often keep your mind occupied during what would otherwise be time spent doing nothing. Instead of letting your brain wander freely, you will focus your thoughts and try to recreate the picture of the latest board setup in your mind.

25. Visiting new places

Just as you can use the time spent at work to develop your memory and mental capacities further, you can utilize your leisure time as well. Regardless of whether it is just a weekend or a full-scale vacation, you need to find good ways to spend it that will also help your mental synapses develop. Spending hours sleeping, doing nothing, or just watching TV will not do much for you. All these activities put your brain to sleep, so to say.

Instead of indulging in these ordinary everyday activities we are all so used to, numerous others can do wonders for your brain. One of them is visiting as many new places and meeting as many new people as possible.

Traveling around the world can really widen your horizons and create numerous new impressions for your brain to store. By visiting new countries, you will be exposed to whole new cultures, including their cuisine, clothing, songs, language, and so much more. These novel sensations are certain to pique your brain's interest.

If you can, try and stay away from large tourist packages. While traveling in big groups has its merits as well, doing it alone or just with the partner will give you many more opportunities to meet the local people and visit different places that are a bit "off the map." These places are often much more intriguing and magical than your common variety tourist destinations.

26. Camping

Even if you can't afford to go traveling for whatever reason, there is no excuse to stay at home and watch TV. Taking a camping trip is a great way to allow yourself to experience the unexpected. Without the help of modern technologies and left to your own means, you will no doubt encounter many interesting situations which will light up your brain like an electric bulb. From building / setting up the place to stay to starting a fire and perhaps even catching your dinner. A good camping trip will indeed create a long lasting impression in your mind.

27. Go for a random ride

Most people get in their cars with some sort of purpose: getting to work, your vacation destination, visiting a friend, etc. But getting in a car and just driving around without any particular goal can be a great experience which is certain to activate different centers in your brain.

You can pick a final destination that you've never visited before or just drive around for as long as you feel like it. Try to take a direction that you usually don't take so to ensure you will experience a lot of novel sights, smells, and sounds.

This will also boost your imagination as you will be actively trying to guess what comes next. Driving through areas that are completely unfamiliar to you will keep your mind active and occupied at all times.

28. Improvisation

One great way to both keep your mind active and actually have fun doing it, is improvisation. There are many things you can do that belong to this section, but here are a few ideas.

Record a part or your favorite show and then write your own funny script for the characters. Have you and your friends sit around and read the dialogue as the recording runs without sound. You can even do this with an animal show if you are imaginative.

You can also make an entirely new video. Today at least, recording a short video is not that big of a deal since every smartphone comes with a camera that should do the trick just fine. Visit a place you like and record it coupled with your commentary. You can talk about some facts you know but also make sure to include some of your personal thoughts and feelings.

29. Pick up a new hobby

We all have things that interest us that we would like to know more about, but for one reason or another, we keep postponing these interests for some other time. Don't. Start a new hobby today.

Every new activity is almost guaranteed to develop particular centers in your brain, but certain hobbies are more beneficial for your mind than the others. One good example is fly fishing, because it requires you to think in a completely different than what you are used to. To catch a fish, you need to think like the fish and predict its movements.

Another good activity would be learning to touch-type. Despite spending a lot of time in front of computers, many people are not very skillful with the keyboard. Learning touch-typing will be convenient as it will increase your typing speed but it will also engage numerous areas of your brain as it requires synchronization of different senses.

30.Cultivating a garden

Another great way to keep your mind occupied is growing and maintaining a garden. The size and the type of plants you cultivate don't matter that much - you can pick anything you prefer or have conditions for. The important thing is that gardening will activate all your senses and activate numerous areas of your brain as you try to figure out the plan and take care of your plants.

Chapter 10
Effective Learning Skills

In this chapter, we will take a look at some proven skills to improve your learning experience. Using them, you will consistently maximize your retention and your understanding of the subject matter.

Skill #1: Reduce Interference

Interference is one cause of forgetting things. Whenever some previously learned information interferes with what you're trying to learn at a time, it's called interference. It causes confusion, and you end up mixing information from both the sources.

Here are some strategies to counter interference.

Overlearning

You are much less likely to mess up the information in your head if you know the material from at least one of the sources well. Continue studying past the point where you can barely recall information and you'll step into the realm of overlearning.

If you're learning a speech, don't just recite it to yourself once. Read it over and over until you can flawlessly recite it without breaking a sweat. That's when you know you've achieved mastery. This considerably reduces interference from other sources.

Avoid studying similar subjects together

If you try to study similar subjects without any intervals, your brain will muddle up information more often. So avoid studying similar subjects together or in close succession. For example, if you have to study geometry, organic chemistry and biochemistry over the next couple of days, space out organic chemistry and biochemistry and study geometry in between. It will avoid possible interferences.

Different rooms for different subjects

If you study different subjects of similar nature in different rooms, it will greatly reduce chances of interference. This is a proven method and works great when you need to understand and remember the different contexts for different subjects. A similar trick is using different colored inks for both subjects. These are just ways to create distinctions between the two subjects as they help the brain associate different elements to these two subjects. Recalling information becomes easier this way because the brain has different hooks for them both.

Bonus: If you're using an image-based memory technique as we discussed in a previous chapter, try and create different mental rooms for both subjects. Include a subject anchor in your images that you can associate to the subjects. For example, if you're learning Spanish and French, start your French mind palace with the Eiffel Tower and your Spanish mind palace with a sombrero.

Skill #2: Use a Study System

While learning something, using a study system is possibly the best thing you can do. Study systems are standard methods of approaching study material, and they greatly boost your performance. There are a number of study systems that have been created over the years, but SQ3R is one of the oldest and most-respected systems out there.

SQ3R is actually an acronym. It includes the steps involved in the system: Survey, Question, Read, Recite, and Review. Let's see how you can perform each step:

Survey

When surveying, your aim is to understand the framework of the study material without going too deep into the details. Read the main parts of the text to have an idea of the structure of the information. Create a mental outline without digging too deep. Reading the table of contents, the preface, and chapter summaries is generally a great idea. Go over headlines and captions, and don't skip the photos. Just skip any actual study material.

Question

Ask yourself questions about each part of the text once you're done surveying it. The questions can be specific or broad, but they should be about the topics you just glazed over. The aim is to keep yourself engaged and interested in the material. You will be thinking deeply about what's to come even before you have actually studied it, which is great for your learning experience.

Read

This is the section most average people start at. They jump into the main material from the get go. But it's important for you to remember that unless you perform the first two steps, you won't make the best out of this step. Surveying and asking questions ensures that the information you're taking in your brain is stored in an orderly manner.

During your first pass, save time and browse through it quickly. Don't take any notes and make sure you use speed-reading techniques. You'll increase your comprehension in the long run.

Don't underline or highlight any text during the first pass either. You have no idea what's important, so discuss it with your peers first.

Recite

Once you've read the text, go through it again and read each heading. Ask questions based on those headings and subheadings, and then answer them yourselves without looking at the book. If you want to remember specific facts, recite them out loud. It improves your memory.

Review

This is the last step and should take you just minutes. Recite your way through the material again, and space out your review sessions. Reviewing the material multiple times ensures it will stay in your memory, so always remember to review before closing the book.

Skill #3: Space It Out

It's important to space out your studying when you're studying a specific subject. It is much more beneficial to finish a chapter in three 1-hour sessions than in one 3-hour session. You might just get away with cramming and do okay in the test next day, but you won't really have learned something unless you space out your learning.

Your attention span is limited and it's difficult to focus on anything for too long. As your study session extends longer, your concentration levels sink with each passing minute. This leads to poor recollection.

Instead, if you take breaks between study sessions, your brain will have time to rest and parse the information recently stored. It will strengthen your memory during the breaks.

You should be careful, however, on how you structure and space out your study sessions. Three 50-minute sessions with breaks of 10 minutes sounds good, but six 25-minute sessions with breaks of 10 minutes sounds completely impractical and ineffective. Time your sessions wisely, using shorter sessions for harder subjects and longer ones for subjects you find relatively easy.

Conclusion

We have covered a lot of different topics in this book. We have busted some popular memory myths and learned how to improve our memory by using different memory techniques. We have also learned what brain fog is and how we can combat it by following a healthy lifestyle. We have learned about some pretty unconventional exercises and tips for improving brain function. All of this will help you slow down cognitive decline and make the most out of your brain's potential. Remember to keep practicing because this is a slow process and it takes time to master some of the systems mentioned here. Do further research and never give up.

In the next pages, you'll find a preview of by book *"Chakras: Your Shortcut To Happiness!"*.

Do you want to feel amazing and live without worries? Happiness and fulfillment are within your grasp, but sometimes just out of reach. You have the power to feel amazing every day of your life. You can radiate energy and feel happy about yourself. You want to be carefree about the things outside of your control, living life to the fullest and having complete control over your emotions. That's what Chakras can and WILL do for you.

Thank you for reading this book!

Robert Capital

Preview of Chakras: *Your Shortcut to Happiness!*

Facts About the Major Chakras

You have been told in the previous chapter that there are seven chakras in your body and every chakra is also associated with a certain organ in your body that is extremely vital for your existence. This chapter gives you certain facts that will help you understand your chakras better than before.

Root Chakra

The root chakra is also called the muladhara chakra that is located at the base of your spine and is the primitive chakra. The environment, your body and the earth have a lovely bond that has is formed due to the root chakra which is the root to your very being. It also helps in keeping you grounded to the earth. You will find that the chakra helps in playing an extremely significant role in keeping you alive!

The chakra helps in keeping you alive since the chakra helps you in deciding whether or not you need to fight or flee if you were in a dangerous situation. The chakra is associated with an aspect that is ancient and is fundamental and also acts as the center of attention to represent animal behavior. This chakra works wonders when you are in a difficult or a tiring time. You will find that this chakra provides you with courage and also the will to survive these difficult times.

The energy that is in this chakra has been transferred from one generation to the next. This energy has been transferred from your ancestors based on the experiences they have had during their lifetime. The root chakra is the base for every chakra and is extremely important for the existence and the balance of every other chakra. It contains every memory that each one of your ancestors may have had with respect to challenges, combats, starvation or any natural disasters. There are certain memories that have been gathered during these experiences that have been stored in the root chakra. These memories get attached to your body in a way they never would have had this chakra not existed. The memories help in creating a bond and a pattern with your ancestors. When you are on your path to uncovering your hidden self, you will be making changes to your life.

You have to remember that every chakra in the body is connected to each other. If there is a change in one chakra, there will definitely be a change in the other chakras. It is essential that you learn how to balance your chakras in order to function on a regular basis. The important thing to remember is that your root chakra is important to ensure that you grow and transform!

Sacral Chakra

The sacral chakra, also called the Svadhisthana, is the chakra that is right after the root chakra. It is the base and the essence of pleasure and passion. This chakra is found in your pelvic areas and is like the command center for every ounce of pleasure you may feel during your lifetime. This chakra, unlike the root chakra, helps you enjoy yourself more and will help you when you are looking for ways to find pleasure. Any feeling or emotion you may be feeling is governed by the sacral chakra. If you are looking at forming a bond with your emotions, sensuality or even intimacy, you will need to balance the energy in this chakra.

The sacral chakra generates energy that will help in letting your emotions lose and also helps in making any changes to your body when you are trying to make a move. The main challenge you would face when there is an imbalance in the energy in the chakras is that you will have opinions that would disappoint the society. You will find it difficult to stick to the norm even when the chakra is balanced, but it is worse when the chakra is imbalanced. The society does not value adjectives and words that describe passion, emotion or feeling. You and every other human being has been trained right from birth that you should never disrupt the rules that have been stated in the society and will always need to be in control. This will always create a lasting impact on your behavior and will make you feel disconnected from your body.

There are certain topics in the society that have been stated as those which can never be discussed in public although it is claimed that this is a modern society. This is because hypocrisy is becoming one of the most popular qualities of the people in the society. This leaves every person with a negative impact and also creates an aversion towards sexuality. It is because of all these issues that people have had a lot of problems with pleasure and enjoyment in their lives. The chakra also helps in enhancing your creativity and will also help you in developing an interest in various forms of art. This is because of the fact that all the emotions have been generated in the sacral chakra. The energy that is found in this chakra is extremely important since it leaves you passionate and sensual. It will also help you in becoming extremely creative!

Solar plexus Chakra

The solar plexus chakra, also called the Manipuri chakra is the third chakra. It is found in between the solar plexus and your navel. Your personality traits identify and ego are often influenced by the energies in this chakra. This is a chakra that helps you identify and understand a perspective of yourself. The energy in this chakra always controls your self – esteem, self – discipline and your will power. When this chakra is balanced well with the energy and is vibrant you will find yourself feeling confident, responsible and more reliable. If there is any dormant energy that is in this chakra, you will find that it has been transformed into action and in movement! You will find that the solar plexus chakra always works towards providing your body with the zeal and the energy to move ahead. The only problem you may face is to be unable to understand how you can use this energy.

The energy that is in this chakra and has been generated in this chakra is extremely strong and is inconsistent. Every individual will react differently to the energy that has been generated in this chakra. You will find that you are stressed out which would leave you with high levels of stress. If the energy in the chakra is blocked, you will find yourself extremely inactive and passive. For a person whose solar plexus is balanced, you will find them with great levels of confidence. These people will always be able to achieve everything they want to in life and will always have the ability to make the right decisions. If there is an imbalance in the chakra, you will need to identify the right ways to ensure that you improve yourself.

The solar plexus chakra helps in providing you with the ability to make the right decisions and will also help you to choose the right path. The chakra will help you in enhancing your self – esteem. But, when you do something negative, you will find your solar plexus chakra also being affected negatively. You will be able to balance the chakra well if you begin to appreciate yourself.

Heart Chakra

The heart chakra, also called the Anahata is the fourth chakra that is found in your body. This chakra is located near your heart and is closely attached with comfort, love, warmth and compassion. This chakra is always responsible for any feelings you may have with respect to love and friendship. It also helps you with creating and maintaining the bonds you form with other individuals. You will also be able to manage emotions like affection, respect, compassion, empathy, apathy and generosity. This chakra plays a major role in helping you maintaining relationships. The color green represents this color making it the color of love. This is the color that has the power to help any person become better. You will find that the chakra helps in providing you with a holistic way to approach and live your life. You will find that your life is larger than you alone! You will be able to develop the ability to love and will also be able to provide yourself with support to maintain a healthy relationship with people you love. When the energy in this chakra is balanced, you will be able to become more sociable and will also be able to understand relationships better. Make sure that you work well towards keeping the energy in this chakra balanced.

Throat Chakra

The fifth chakra or the throat chakra is the starting point of every chakra in the body. It is also called the Vishuddha chakra and is found near your neck. It expands towards your shoulders and all across your neck to be very precise. The color associated with this chakra is blue and this is the center for every ounce of creativity that is in your body.

The energy that is generated in this chakra manifests itself into certain talents that are in you. You will be able to connect with your inner self and will also be able to find a connection with the Cosmos or the divine self.

Blue always represents a color that is free of any hindrances and is extremely pure. The path that you can travel on in order to adopt hope and faith is always guided by this color. There are other colors you have found in the chakras above that will have a different impact on your body. When the throat chakra is full of energy and is balanced well, you will find yourself having numerous positive impacts. You will find yourself feeling calm and composed and will also be able to be at peace with yourself and every other entity around you. If the energy in the chakra is weak or imbalanced, you will become nervous and irritable. You may become an introvert and a poor listener.

The insights to your creativity are always responsible to provide you with the zeal and the drive to create something new and this is provided by this chakra. You will find that it gets difficult to create something out of nothing, but when this chakra is balanced, you will be able to make a conscious decision. You will need to work on the creativity that is inside your body and use that to help you with the process of making something new. It is always good to use your talents to your benefit.

Third Eye Chakra

This is the sixth chakra out of the seven major chakras that you have in your body. This chakra is also called the ajna chakra and is found right between your eyebrows and right above your nose. This chakra provides you with the knowledge to be able to transcend between the boundaries of the mortal world that would help you connect with the cosmos. This implies that you and every other individual will always be able to see both the mortal world and the outer world.

This chakra is often associated with indigo, which is also referred to as royal blue. The chakra represents a vast amount of wisdom, knowledge and the awareness of a person's inner self. The color is a very dark shade of blue and is always associated with night and helps in unlocking the door that helps you approach the realm of divinity. The energies in the other chakras can be combined with the third eye chakra in order to attain greater levels of divinity and spirituality. This is something you will need to do with caution. This is because of the fact that you have to always ensure that you maintain a connection with the world while trying to attain a greater level of wisdom.

If you are someone who is getting extremely involved with the other dimensions, you will not be of any use since you will find yourself getting too detached from everyone or everything you may hold extremely dear to you. Just like every other chakra, you will find that you an imbalance in this chakra would affect you extremely badly. If there is any negative energy in your chakra, you will find yourself listening to voices or even having nightmares. You will become impulsive and may even become very obsessed or delusional. When the energy in this chakra has been balanced well, you will find yourself peaceful, intuitive and perceptive. You will begin to make the right decisions with a clear mind and will also be able to maintain positive traits for the rest of your life.

Crown Chakra

This is the last chakra in your body and is one of the most important chakras of all! The crown chakra is also called the Sahara chakra and is located at the crown area of an individual. The color associated with this chakra is violet and the energies in the chakra would help an individual experience life to the fullest. They will be able to identify the best things about their life without any external help and will also be able to understand the happiness gained from the tiniest things that happen in life.

When the person understands this, they will have the ability to be at peace with themselves and with the people around them. The energy that is found in this chakra will help in acting as the unifying force that will help you in understanding the association you may have with the Cosmos. Every question that you may have ever had about your life or destiny can be answered with the energy that is in the chakra. There are certain things that may have bothered you initially will begin to seem extremely petty. You will find that it is easy to let go of these issues and understand what the meaning of your life is.

The information given in this chapter covers the seven major chakras that are all found in the body. You have also been told about how these chakras have been associated with the different organs in your body. The chakras are all very important and if you find that one chakra is imbalanced, every other chakra will follow. It is extremely important that you do not give one chakra more importance when compared to any other chakra. The chakras are all associated with a color in the rainbow. The chakras have to always be in complete harmony with each other. If there is absolutely no harmony between the chakras, you will notice the trouble starting. In the latter chapters, you will learn more about the different processes you will need to use in order to balance the energies in the chakras.

It is extremely important to be patient. You have to read through every chapter carefully and understand every minute detail that has been mentioned throughout the book. You will need to ensure that you just do not acquire the knowledge but will also have to understand the depth of the words that have been use d in the book. That will be the only way you will be able to attain a certain level of equilibrium.

Discover different easy techniques to open and balance your chakras today!

You can find "Chakras: Your Shortcut To Happiness

Or you can go to: http://amzn.to/1OpVnZ3

Made in the USA
Middletown, DE
24 September 2017